Flea Goes the Football

Written by Jill Eggleton
Illustrated by Astrid Matijasevich

Big Bill and Flea were
at the football.
The Squits were playing
the Jumbos.

Big Bill liked the Squits.
But when he saw
the Jumbos, he said . . .

"**Wow!**
The little Squits won't win!"

The Jumbos were
very big.
They looked down
at the little Squits and
they laughed.

Hee- hee- hee!

"You are **so** little!
You won't win this game!"
they said . . .

and they ran off
with the ball.

Big Bill jumped
up and down.

"Come on, Squits!"
he shouted.
"You must get the ball!"

But the Squits
couldn't get the ball
from the Jumbos.

Flea went

hop, hop, hop

onto the field.

Jumbo Two got the ball.
Flea went

hop, hop, hop

on his leg.

"**Ouch!**" shouted Jumbo Two,
and he let the ball go.

The Squits ran to the goal.

"A goal to the Squits!"
called Big Bill.

Jumbo Six got the ball.

Flea went

hop, hop, hop

on his leg.

"**Ouch!**" shouted Jumbo Six,
and he let the ball go.

The Squits got
a goal again.

When the game was over,
the Squits had ten goals
and the Jumbos had two.

The Jumbos looked down
at the Squits.

"What were we doing?"
they said.
"You are so little, but we
couldn't keep the ball."

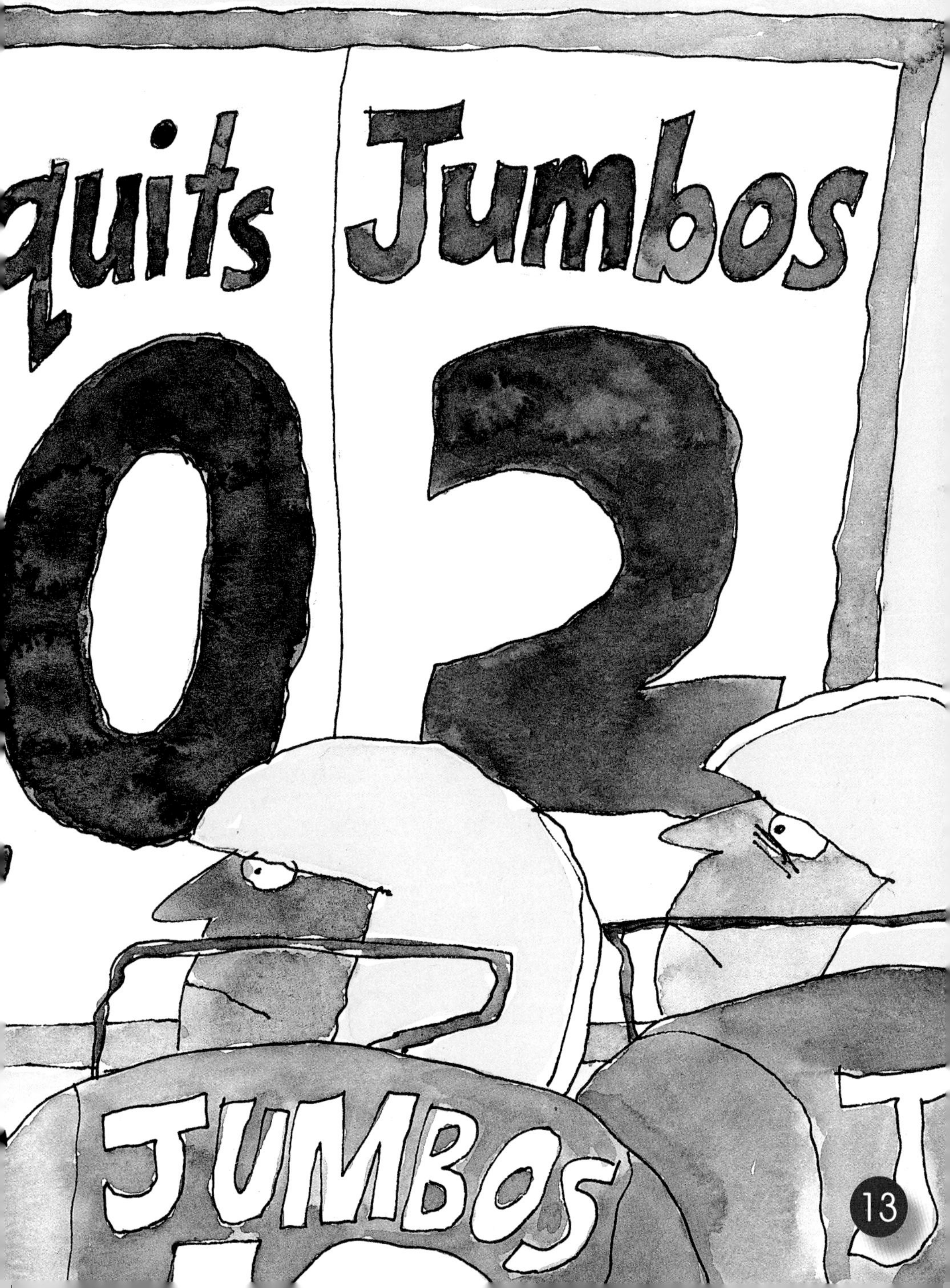
quits
Jumbos
0
2
JUMBOS

The Squits laughed.
"Little is cool," they said.

And up on Big Bill's hat . . .
Flea went

hop, hop, hop.

An Action/Consequence Chart

Guide Notes

Title: Flea Goes to the Football
Stage: Early (4) – Green

Genre: Fiction
Approach: Guided Reading
Processes: Thinking Critically, Exploring Language, Processing Information
Written and Visual Focus: Action/Consequence Chart, Thought Bubble, Speech Bubbles
Word Count: 224

THINKING CRITICALLY
(sample questions)
- What do you think this story could be about? Look at the title and discuss.
- Look at the cover. What do you think Flea is going to do at the football?
- Look at pages 2 and 3. Why do you think Big Bill said, "The little Squits won't win"?
- Look at pages 4 and 5. How do you think the Squits felt when the Jumbos told them they wouldn't win the game?
- Look at pages 6 and 7. What do you think the Squits could do to get the ball from the Jumbos?
- Look at pages 10 and 11. How do you think the Squits feel now?
- Look at pages 12 and 13. Why do you think Flea wanted to help the Squits?

EXPLORING LANGUAGE

Terminology
Title, cover, illustrations, author, illustrator

Vocabulary
Interest words: football, goal, field
High-frequency words: won't, must, couldn't, called, keep
Positional words: up, down, onto, on, off, over
Compound words: football

Print Conventions
Capital letter for sentence beginnings and names (**B**ig **B**ill, **F**lea, **S**quits, **J**umbo **T**wo, **J**umbo **S**ix), full stops, commas, exclamation marks, quotation marks, question mark, ellipsis, possessive apostrophe